Stephen Curry

The Life Story of One of the World's Greatest
Basketball Players

By Jayson Morris

Table of Contents

Introduction

Stephen Curry has always been regarded as a prodigy who inherited the skill of basketball from his father and mentor, Dell Curry. He's one of the most successful shooters to ever play in the NBA and, in 2014-15, he won the NBA Most Valuable Player Award. It was his hard work and determination which led the Golden State Warriors to their first championship since 1975.

Curry has always had basketball in his genes but he took what his father gave him to another level by honing his skills as a shooter. He played basketball from a very young age and was trained by his father. He went on to play basketball for Davidson College and achieved numerous records while he was there.

Stephen Curry has achieved countless NBA records for three-pointers and currently holds the record for the most three-pointers made in a single season. Curry has had a difficult life and it was his struggle that got him where he is right now.

This book will tell you all about the life of basketball legend Stephen Curry and how he became the person that he is today. Thank you for buying this book and I hope that you enjoy reading it.

Chapter 1: Early Life

"Doesn't matter where you come from, what you have or don't have... All you need to have is faith in God, and undying passion for what you do, what you choose to do in this life, and a relentless drive and the will to do whatever it takes to be successful at whatever you put your mind to."

Stephen Curry

Wardell Stephen Curry II was born on March 14 1988, in Akron, Ohio to Sonya and Dell Curry, while his father Dell was still playing for the Cleveland Cavaliers. Allegedly, Curry and LeBron James were born under the same roof, on the same floor and in the same decade but just 39 months apart. So, Curry has way more in common with the legendary LeBron James than just basketball.

Curry grew up in Charlotte, North Carolina while his father was playing for the Charlotte Hornets. He had a connection with basketball from a very young age and used to accompany his dad to all his games. He was named after his grandfather Jack. Stephen also inherited the same basket that his father got from Jack. Stephen had an incredibly sporty background at home in Ohio, surrounded by two professional athletes, his parents – Dell and Sonya Curry – who gave him much of his athletic inspiration. But that household did not stay in Ohio very long. His father's career made the family move to various parts of North America – from Ohio to Canada to North Carolina.

Childhood and Upbringing

Stephen Curry grew up attending a Christian Montessori school that was started by his mother. Believe it or not, attending a school like that was a big reason that the Curry family grew very close to each other. The Curry siblings all went to school together with their mom, grandmother and aunt. It was in this school that Stephen first learned about independence and accountability. Sonya was also a very strict disciplinarian. Stephen remembered that on the night before his first middle school game, he purposely skipped washing the dishes. As a consequence, his mother did not allow him to play.

Even though both parents were successful athletes, playing sports was not the priority in the Curry household. The children in the Curry family were clear with the priorities in their life – faith, family and academics – (in that order) were above everything else, including sports. Sonya explained that they did not pressure their children to pursue an athletic career like many other ex-athlete parents. They had observed that many sons of ex-athletes thought that their only path in life was to become athletes themselves, and did not know what else to do as a consequence.

She elaborated that they only wanted their children to be "normal and grounded." Stephen is very grateful to his parents and other relatives because of the way they raised him. He adds that he and his siblings were very blessed to have such great influences in their lives while growing up.

Stephen recalls that, although he watched a lot of his dad's games when he was young, the best games for him as a child were the ones between him and his little brother, Seth. They used to play non-stop into the night in their backyard until their mom would yell for both of them to come inside. But little did the brothers know that they would both play in front of national audiences soon.

Early Basketball Experience

Being the son of a former NBA shooting guard, Stephen Curry had the ideal platform on which to learn and grow into the brilliant sharpshooter that he has become. Since his younger days, Stephen has always been a basketball fanatic and lover.

His father, Dell Curry, speaks of how Stephen was at his first basketball game when he was only two weeks old. It is evident that Stephen learned how to play the game by watching his father Dell in action. Dell Curry was a career 40% shooter from the three-point line in his NBA career. He made more than 1,200 three-point shots and was regarded as one of the best shooters in the NBA.

The younger Curry, as a child, during visits to his

grandparents' house in Grottoes, Virginia, would also spend time shooting baskets at that hoop. Some shots were even further than his father had shot in his childhood. That was when Stephen Curry started to fall for the long jump shot.

The days spent playing in Grandpa Jack's makeshift basket helped the young Curry as well. Not only was Stephen's shooting honed by trying to get the ball straight through the hoop of Jack's basket, but his ball-handling skills were also developed as he dribbled through the rough terrain of the grandparents' yard. He had to dribble creatively to avoid rocks and other obstacles on his way to the basket. Moreover, he also had to make sure the ball hit precisely through the basket because the yard was always muddy. He had to keep the ball clean at all times, and that was the only way to prevent the basketball from getting mud all over it. When finishing layups, the makeshift backboard did not give him any breaks.

Stephen had to learn how to finish at certain angles to solve the test of the backboard. He would even listen to how his dad and his grandpa would argue and discuss shot fundamentals and basics, as Dell was already an NBA player in those days. Though he did all that at a young age, that was when everything started for Stephen Curry.

Jack died from a heart attack in 1991. Though Stephen would still go back to his grandparents' home in Grottoes, he spent most of his days shooting on his family's half court at their home in Charlotte. That court was made out of concrete, and the basket was NBA grade.

However, Stephen Curry hated it until he reached high school because he was so used to playing in Grottoes, where the yard had a lot of obstacles and the hoop was a challenge to shoot at.

Before his days in the NBA, Curry found himself playing very well at the middle school level while the family was living in Canada. His father was playing for the Toronto Raptors between 2001 and 2002. Stephen Curry was going to Queensway Christian College in Etobicoke, Ontario, Canada, for his seventh- and eighth-grade school years and helped the Saints team find success during those two years.

When he was in Toronto, Curry often watched his father's games live. Of course, the main attraction was the high-flying Vince Carter. But Stephen knew how to pay attention to the minute details of the game. He was only 14 years old at that time and was the main superstar for Queensway Christian College. In those days, he was a small, scrawny boy but was the team's leading player. During one Raptors game, the camera crew had a chance to talk to the adolescent Stephen.

Stephen said what every consummate professional athlete should always say. He told the crew that he wanted to make it to the NBA by practicing and working hard. At that time, he was a small sized boy.

While smaller athletes could get away with their size through their athleticism, Stephen was not even an explosive youngster back then. He was simply a player that scored a lot of points by working hard on his shot and by utilizing the fundamentals in the right way.

One of his teachers recalled how the younger Curry impressed everyone with high games of 40 and 50 points that seemed so natural for the son of the Raptors' star and helped the Saints team go undefeated in the 2001-02 season.

There really was not a close challenger in the area after they defeated Mentor College in a tournament championship game in which they were down by 8 points with only about a minute left. The Toronto Star had a story about finding some of Curry's former teachers and coaches at the school who could remember that he asked them to give him the ball, so they did, resulting in a flurry of three-point field goals and steals, causing a 13-point swing that gave the Saints the win.

In addition to that, Curry continued to develop his game from beyond the three-point line not only in youth basketball at the middle school level but also through a club team, the Toronto 5-0, that competed in many places. While basketball was created in the United States, Canada has provided plenty of talent of its own and Curry saw some of that in games against other players he would later meet in the NBA. In fact, the Toronto 5-0's biggest rivals were the Scarborough Blues and Curry faced off against Cory Joseph and Kelly Olynyk.

However, Curry returned to the U.S. and found himself back in Charlotte, North Carolina, where his father had his best years in the NBA.

Chapter 2: High School

"Success is not an accident, success is actually a choice."

Stephen Curry

Stephen attended the Charlotte Christian School in Charlotte, North Carolina. He did not waste any time showcasing his skills as a premier and professional caliber basketball player. As someone who stood only about 5'6" and weighed just 125 pounds at the age of 15, Curry was a freshman called up from the junior varsity team during a state tournament game against Ravenscroft in 2003. There was not much to look at, literally, as the jersey could have been mistaken for a nightgown on the very young Curry. With his team losing by double digits, Curry brought the ball down the court and confidently took a step up to a three-point attempt that hit nothing but net.

That was when Coach Shonn Brown knew that the

future of the Knights' basketball program and the game plan moving forward were going to revolve around Curry. But what people do not know is how Stephen Curry developed into a great high school player. At that time, he was a 5'6" skinny teenager, who had all the skills and the work ethic to play professionally, but whose fundamentals were dead wrong. Dell Curry noticed that when the family was in Grottoes. He saw how his son shot the ball from his hip. Stephen had been shooting the ball that way ever since he was a young boy. It was an ugly shot, but he was making it at a high rate. But Dell did not like it. He knew that longer and more athletic players could easily block the shot. The elder Curry made his son rebuild his shooting form from scratch.

Naturally, Stephen Curry did what his father told him to do. However, it was not all that easy. Stephen worked hard on changing his shot in the family's half court basket in Charlotte. Those were some of the lowest months of Stephen's life. At that time, he even hated shooting.

Before Dell talked him into rebuilding his shot,

Stephen was a consummate workhorse. Other NBA players worked on their form by shooting hundreds of jump shots every day. On the other hand, the sophomore high school player Stephen Curry made sure he shot a thousand jumpers every day. But, he hated shooting while he was trying to retool his form. Dell would even say that Stephen was shooting with teary eyes that summer. But the young Curry manned up through it all because he wanted to make to the professional leagues. He wanted to be the best, and he had to do what was needed to get there.

After that summer, Stephen Curry had perfected the shot he has used countless of times to drain thousands of three-pointers in today's NBA. Months of hard work paid dividends as his quick release low-lift jump shot was shaped.

At that time, changing a hip jump shot into a low-lift high-arcing jumper was a good idea for any shooter. But Dell and Stephen did not know that the shot they both worked on so hard during the whole summer of Stephen's sophomore season would turn out to be the deadliest weapon the

NBA has ever seen.

After that season, Curry continued to play well for his high school team. Stephen received many awards including the all-state, all-conference, and team MVP (Most Valuable Player) awards. He was a three-time letter winner and accumulated a total of 1,400 points in his career for a school record, which gave him an average of about 18 points per game. Charlotte Christian won three conference championships during Curry's run with the team, and that included three appearances in the North Carolina state tournament.

During Curry's senior season, he made 48 percent of his field goals as the offensive star for the Knights. They finished the season 33-3 and were the state runners-up in 2006 after losing 61-53 to Greensboro Day on February 25, 2006. It was still a good run for Curry, who also had a chance to finish his high school career on the same court as his younger brother Seth for two of those seasons.

Leaving High School and College Disappointment

Perhaps the most shocking incident after his tremendous success in high school was that he was not offered a single scholarship from a major conference school, even though he rightfully deserved one because of his 48 percent shooting percentage from behind the arc.

Most scouts and coaches from the major programs dismissed him as being "too skinny" or "too short" to make an impact in college basketball. Stephen was only 6 feet tall and weighed 180 pounds when he was a high school senior, prompting these remarks. Because of his lack of size and athleticism, not a lot of colleges were interested in Stephen Curry. At that point, countless hours used to develop the perfect jump shot were almost put to waste because none of the big college programs wanted a skinny, un-athletic 6 footer in their lineup.

He was only rated as a three-star recruit and did not make the national top 100 - 150 recruits lists on sports websites such as ESPN and Rivals. One scout even gave him a very low score of 36 out of 100 in his personal evaluation.

Eric Bossi was one of the national scouts from Rivals who was not impressed with Curry's high school numbers and stated that he was too short and skinny to be able to be an active player for any of the big collegiate programs. He was considered good enough to make open shots without many misses and not many matched his passing, ball handling, and work ethic.

The problem was that a lot of programs and college scouts could not see what Curry's full potential would be if he grew a little taller, added some more weight, and had some time to mature and improve his overall basketball ability. That was a big reason that a lot of programs in the Atlantic Coast Conference would not even offer a chance for Curry to walk on to fight for a roster spot.

Nonetheless, Stephen entertained some mid-major options. In reality, he wanted to go to Virginia

Tech because of his father's hall of fame status there, but he was not offered a scholarship by the school. The Hokies only extended an invitation to him as a walk-on, and he would not have any money to pay for school outside of academic scholarships. Curry would also be placed in redshirt status, which would give him a year to prove he was worth bringing onto the team while preserving a year of college eligibility. It would also be a riskier play in an attempt to get on the team in the first place while losing years of eligibility. That was why Curry chose to go a different route for playing college basketball. Virginia Tech head coach Seth Greenberg would later go on to say that he did offer Curry a spot, but not a full scholarship as several players had earlier agreed to play for them.

No major college program ever offered Stephen a place on their roster. The schools that did offer the young Stephen Curry a scholarship were the Davidson Wildcats, Virginia Commonwealth (VCU) Rams, and the Winthrop Eagles – all mid-major programs. He chose Davidson because he liked its tightly knit community located in Davidson, North Carolina, which features a total enrollment below 2,000 students and a good education.

Having said that, Stephen went on to work wonders for Davidson College, which had not won a single title game since 1969. Not being offered a scholarship by his father's alma mater was depressing, but it became motivation for the young Curry; the motivation that turned out to be ideal for the small basketball program at Davidson that was hoping to build from their first-round loss to Minnesota as the 15-seed in the 2006 NCAA National Championship Tournament.

Chapter 3: College Years

"What I tell people is be the best version of yourself in anything that you do. You don't have to live anybody else's story."

Stephen Curry

Stephen Curry played at Davidson College for three years. In that period, he made a massive impact and propelled the Wildcats to many great performances. He turned out to be their star player. Curry picked up right where he left off from his high school days and went up from there, improving drastically year after year. His numbers kept getting better, and he had some moments that would be remembered for a long time.

Coming into his first college season, the name "Stephen Curry" was hardly known. Of course, he was not even highly recruited in his final year in high school. As mentioned, Curry was not even ranked among the best high school players in the country. Despite the initial setbacks Curry faced, he was a determined player.

Many players would fold under the disappointment of not having a chance to play for a big college program. Stephen was not a one of them. Of course, it also helped a lot that he had several firm believers ready to push him to become a better player. Other than his family, Davidson head coach Bob McKillop saw the makings of what could be the school's best player in its history. He did not mind what other schools said about Stephen. Sure, Curry was skinny and frail. But McKillop saw a good fighter in Curry. He was the type of player that would get up eight times after falling seven times. His heart and his resiliency were qualities no other top-ranked prep star had.

Freshman Year

Despite the faith that McKillop had in his freshman player, he kicked Stephen out of the gym on his first day of practice. Curry was late that day. After that, he never came in late. The only time he would be late was when it was time to leave the practice facility. Stephen was always the last one to leave, as he spent hours honing his craft. In his first year at Davidson, Curry made an immediate impact and laid the foundation for his future success.

In his first game of the season on the road at Eastern Michigan on November 10, 2006, Curry went 5 of 12 from the field (41.7 percent) and 3 of 7 from three-point range (42.9 percent) to score 15 points while collecting 5 rebounds, 3 assists, and 3 steals in an 81-77 win. The one difficult part of the game for Curry was ball control as a point guard since he turned the ball over 13 times to the Eastern Michigan Eagles. Despite that, McKillop refused to lose faith in his recruit. He cut that down the next day on the road against the Michigan Wolverines by turning the ball over just three times. But his offense caught fans' attention in just his second appearance as a freshman in the 78-68 loss to Michigan on November 11, 2006. Curry gave a preview of the dominance that was to come in his near future with a 32-point game, along with 9 rebounds and 4 assists; he shot 48 percent from the field (12 of 25).

Davidson bounced back in the last stop on their season-opening three-game road trip at Central Connecticut State with a 91-64 win on November 12, 2006. Curry made 3 of 5 from behind the three-point arc (60 percent) and 4 of 10 overall for 16 points to go along with 6 rebounds, 5 assists, 3 steals, and 1 block. He was starting to find his offensive stride in the non-conference schedule during a 100-89 win in the home opener against the University of Illinois-Chicago on November 15, 2006. He scored 27 points, shooting 11 of 19 from the field and 3 of 6 from three-point range. Curry then lost some of that momentum by turning the ball over 10 times in an 81-75 loss to the Missouri Tigers of the Southeastern Conference on November 19, 2006, a game in which he shot only 4 of 11 from the field (36.4 percent) for just 16 points, 6 assists, 4 rebounds, and 4 steals.

Davidson began a long winning streak that started in December and most of January after the loss to one of the nation's top programs. It began on December 1, 2006, during an 86-61 win over Elon, in which Curry scored 11 points and continued December 4, 2006, when Curry made 40.9 percent from the field, including 4 of 9 from behind the three-point arc, to score 24 points in a 66-63 win over North Carolina- Greensboro. Curry then scored 17 points, making 50 percent from the field, to help the Wildcats defeat the Charlotte 49ers 79-51 on December 9, 2006. After nearly a week of rest, Davidson got a very convincing 116-55 win over Mount Saint Mary on December 15, 2006, with Curry making 6 of 10 from three-point range (60 percent) and 7 of 11 overall from the field for 20 points to go along with 4 rebounds.

Davidson entered the Southern Conference schedule as one of the favorites to win the conference and possibly earn a spot in the NCAA National Championship tournament. It started off well as the Wildcats' winning streak continued on January 6, 2007, with an 81-73 win over Charleston where Curry made 6 of 16 from the field (2 of 9 from three-point range) to score 19 points to go along with 2 rebounds. His teammate, Thomas Sander, led the team with 25 points and

10 rebounds after making 10 of 14 from the field. Curry scored another 15 points after making 4 of 11 from the field and 6 of 8 from the foul line as the Wildcats defeated Furman, 71-63, on January 10, 2007; once again, Sander led the team with 24 points, followed by Jason Richards' 18 points.

While other players were getting the most points early in the Southern Conference schedule, Curry was still doing well as a developing freshman. He scored another 16 points with 6 rebounds and 4 assists in an 83-78 win over Wofford on January 13, 2007, followed by a team-leading 17 points when he made 5 of 9 from the field (4 of 6 from three-point range) during a 79-54 win over the Citadel on January 16, 2007. Curry also collected 4 rebounds, 3 assists, and 2 steals in that game. Curry and Davidson lost their first conference game of the schedule on January 20, 2007, when Appalachian State defeated the Wildcats at Davidson by a score of 81-74. Curry scored 15 points, but he was able to make only 1 of 11 from behind the three-point arc and just 6 of 17 overall from the field for 35.3 percent. It was the last conference loss for Davidson in a long time, and Curry had a streak of games in which he scored 20 or more points that lasted through most of February. It started with a 101-92 high-scoring affair on January 23, 2007, when Curry scored 23 points by making 7 of 14 from the field, including 4 of 10 from long distance.

Curry then led the team with 25 points, going 8 of 11 from the field (5 of 8 from long range) to help the Wildcats get a 79-59 win over Western Carolina. In the next game, against Elon on January 30, 2007, Curry scored another 25 points by making 9 of 17 from the field while collecting 8 rebounds in an 88-58 blowout win on the road. Curry nearly hit the 30-point mark again in a 75-65 win at home over North Carolina- Greensboro on February 3, 2007, when he scored 29 points. Most of his damage came from converting 7 of 13 from behind the three-point line to help Davidson win their 20th game of the season.

Davidson only had one blemish on their Southern Conference record in the regular season with a record of 14-1 before going into the conference tournament, where the winner would get an automatic bid to the NCAA National Championship tournament. In the first round against Chattanooga on March 1, 2007, Davidson got the 78-68 win when Curry made 6 of 16 from the field (37.5 percent) and only 3 of 11 from three-point range for 20 points, with 5 rebounds, 4 assists, and 3 steals. Twenty-four hours later, on March 2, 2007, Curry had a much better game shooting from long distance at 6 of 10 (60 percent) and 9 of 14 overall from the field (64.3 percent) to lead the team with 30 points, along with 4 rebounds and 2 assists.

In the Southern Conference Championship on March 3, 2007, Curry made 10 of 24 from the field (41.7 percent) and 5 of 7 from the foul line to score 29 points with 8 rebounds in a 72-65 win over Charleston. It was a thrilling game in which Curry played a season-high 40 minutes.

The win gave Davidson a record of 29-4 and the automatic berth in the NCAA tournament. Because of their conference, Davidson was given a 13-seed in the tournament and placed in the Midwest

Regional to face the fourth-seeded Maryland Terrapins, who were given an at-large bid into the tournament after compiling a 24-8 record in the tough Atlantic Coast Conference. In the game played in Buffalo, New York on March 15, 2007, Davidson fell in the first round, 82-70. Curry scored 30 points, making 9 of 21 from the field (42.9 percent) and 5 of 14 from three-point range (35.7 percent), but he fouled out after playing 36 minutes. Richards was the only other player to score in double digits with 11 points. Davidson shot just 34.3 percent from the field with most of the offense coming from their star freshman. He was also an essential part of Davidson being able to earn their first NCAA tournament bid in almost 40 years.

Even though they were eliminated in the first round of the national championship tournament, it was considered a successful season for the Davidson Wildcats with the development of their young star, Curry. The talented freshman averaged 21.5 points per game and played in all 34 of Davidson's games.

Curry's success in his freshman year did not end there, as he was selected to represent the USA at the FIBA Under-19 World Championship, where he excelled again. He was selected as the Southern Conference Freshman of the Year, Tournament MVP, and a member of the all-tournament team, along with many other prestigious awards.

Sophomore Year

In his sophomore year, Stephen Curry had more chances to impress. It started early with a non-conference exhibition against Emory, a 120-56 blowout on November 9, 2007, when Curry made 10 of 15 from the field, with 5 of 8 coming from behind the three-point arc to score 27 points while collecting 7 rebounds and 7 assists. He was the star performer in most of Davidson's matches and stepped up to face stronger teams like North Carolina, North Carolina State, and Duke. Even though the Wildcats lost all of these games by close margins, Curry was the standout player, averaging 24.3 points in these three games along with making some spectacular assists and unselfish plays.

Davidson defeated North Carolina Central 98-50 on November 24, 2007, (Curry scored 16 points), and had an early Southern Conference win over Appalachian State, 71-60, on November 24, 2007 (38 points). In that game, Curry scored 20 points, making 8 of 17 from the field (4 of 7 from behind the three-point arc). He led Davidson in a close 79-73 loss to the Duke Blue Devils, who were undefeated at the time.

After starting the New Year with a nonconference win over Georgia Southern, 92-67, on January 3, 2008 – Curry had a double-double with 24 points and 10 rebounds while making 8 of 19 from the field – Davidson started its conference schedule with major wins. They beat Western Carolina on January 5, 2008, by a score of 86-73 thanks to Curry's team leading 19 points, despite making just 1 of 11 from three-point range. That was followed by a close 59-57 win over Elon on January 9, 2008. In that game, Curry persevered after making just 4 of 15 from the field overall (26.7 percent) and just 2 of 6 from long distance (33.3 percent) to score only 15 points.

Curry had plenty of high-scoring games that made his freshman season look weak in comparison. That did not mean that Curry was always the leading scorer for Davidson, there were others who were starting to step up when their star had a bad shooting night – something they did not have in some of their non-conference games earlier in the season. Thomas Sander led the team with 21 points in the Wildcats' 70-58 win over Charleston on January 26, 2008, a game in which Curry was just 5 of 14 from the field for 16 points and 6 rebounds. But Curry still established himself as one of the best scoring threats in NCAA Division I basketball, which was seen in the team's 78-65 win over Wofford, when he went 11 of 20 and 6 of 12 from three-point range to score 34 points with 5 rebounds, 5 assists, and 2 steals.

One of Curry's most memorable games was when the Davidson Wildcats played against UNC-Greensboro on February 13, 2008. Coming out of halftime with a 20-point deficit, he went off, making 41 points to ultimately defeat UNC-Greensboro, 83-78. Overall, Curry went 14 of 26 from the field, just 4 of 11 from behind the three-point line, and made all 9 free throws. He also collected 7 rebounds and 4 steals in the game. His shooting percentages continued to stay at or above 50 percent for most of the rest of the season. After scoring 26 points with 5 assists during an 86-51 win over Furman on February 16, 2008, Curry scored another 30 points in the rematch against UNC-Greensboro at Davidson on February 19, 2008. Curry was 10 of 18 from the field with 6 of 9 three-pointers to go along with 4 assists and 3 rebounds, helping to give the Wildcats a 75-66 win.

Davidson finished the regular season with an undefeated 17-0 record in conference play and won 19 straight after starting 4-8 in late December. As the regular-season champion, Davidson was the top seed in the Southern Conference tournament that began on March 8, 2008, at home against Wofford, whom the Wildcats defeated 82-49.

After Curry led the Wildcats to a 20-0 Southern Conference record and a 26-6 regular season record, Davidson entered the 2008 NCAA Division I men's basketball tournament as the 10th seed in the Midwest region. They were matched in the first round with the Gonzaga Bulldogs, the seventh seed that had a 25- 7 recording coming out of the West Coast Conference.

In the first round, which was held on March 21, 2008, in Raleigh, North Carolina, Davidson got its first NCAA tournament win since 1969 with an 82-76 victory. Curry was almost perfect as he made 14 of 22 from the field for a field goal percentage of about 64 percent, including 8 of 10 three-point field goals. Curry finished the upset with 40 points, 5 steals, 3 rebounds, and 2 assists.

Next came the match between Davidson and the heavily favored Georgetown Hoyas, who were the second seed after going 27-5 in the Big East Conference. On March 23, 2008, Curry showed tremendous resilience when he brought his team back into the lead after overcoming a 17-point deficit to shockingly defeat Georgetown by 4 points, 74-70. He led the comeback effort with 30 spectacular points, 25 of which came in the second half. By the end of the game, Curry was 8 of 21 from the field and made 9 of 10 from the foul line while also collecting 5 assists, 3 rebounds, and 3 steals. However, Stephen Curry was just getting started with the win over the Hoyas.

In the next round, he overcame the opposition's top defender, Michael Flowers; when he scored 33 points in an easy win over third-seeded Wisconsin by a score of 73-56 in the Sweet Sixteen matchup on March 28, 2008. Curry was much more efficient in this game, shooting 50 percent while making 6 of 11 from behind the three-point arc; Curry also collected 4 steals, 4 assists, and 3 rebounds. This paved the way to Davidson's first Elite Eight appearance since 1969.

In the NCAA Midwest Regional Final on March 30, 2008, Curry pulled out all the stops in an attempt to seal a win, but unfortunately, Davidson fell to the Kansas Jayhawks by 2 points in a low-scoring thriller on March 30, 2008.

Sophomore year was when Stephen Curry began to cement his name in the history books with many significant milestones. With that, he still had not yet finished his career with the Wildcats of Davidson College.

Junior Year

Following his great success in 2008, Curry was prepared to take on the big leagues: the NBA. However, he announced that he would play one last season for Davidson. At that time, players had to be one year removed from high school graduation to be eligible for the NBA's annual rookie draft. But Curry was one of the rare college stars who played beyond their impressive freshman seasons.

Curry wasted no time in preparing for the NBA: Starting on November 14, 2008, during a 107-83 win over Guilford, he had a double-double, scoring 29 points and collecting 10 assists, shooting 9 of 20 from the field (45 percent) and 9 of 10 from the foul line.

Curry was making himself known as one of the nation's best scorers as he showed in a 100-95 victory at home over Chattanooga on December 13,

2008. He converted on 11 of 22 field goals (50 percent) with 5 of 11 from three-point range (45.5 percent) and 14 of 18 from the foul line to finish with 41 points, along with 6 assists and 4 rebounds.

With their focus primarily on the Southern Conference, Davidson traveled to the Citadel for an 84-69 win on January 10, 2009, when Curry made 50 percent from the field (half of his field goals were from behind the three-point line with 4 of 8 converted) and sank 12 of 14 free throws to lead the team with 32 points along with 6 rebounds, 5 assists, and 5 steals as Davidson earned the 78-61 win.

Curry continued to be the focal point of Davidson's offense, earning another double-double with 20 points and 10 rebounds during a 70-49 win over UNC-Greensboro on February 25, 2009. As he continued his junior season, Curry found enormous success. He reached many incredible milestones in a very short period. He surpassed the 2,000-point mark in just 83 games. He also became Davidson College's second-leading scorer in history shortly after that. He did not stop there, as a 34-point game against Georgia Southern during a 99-56 win on February 28, 2009, pushed him ahead of John Gerdy, making him the Wildcats' highest scorer ever. The regular season was concluded with a 90-78 win on the road at Elon on March 2, 2009, when Curry scored 26 points by making 8 of 16 from the field and 8 of 10 on the foul line; Curry also collected 5 assists, 4 steals, and 3 rebounds in that game.

Behind Stephen Curry's leadership, Davidson lost a mere 2 games and won 18 in conference play. Despite their impressive conference record and the lobbying of their coach and even coaches of other programs, Davidson failed to get a slot in the NCAA tournament this time around. In the Southern Conference tournament, Curry scored 43 points in the quarterfinals during an 84-68 win over Appalachian State on March 7, 2009. It was the third-highest that had ever been scored in the conference tournament, thanks to Curry making 11 of 18 from the field (61.1 percent), including 5 of 10 behind the three-point arc, and converting on 16 of

18 from the foul line. But on March 8, 2009, Davidson lost in the Southern Conference semifinals by a score of 59- 52 to Charleston. Curry struggled from long distance, making only 2 of 11 three-point field goals and 5 of 18 from the field overall (27.8 percent) for just 20 points.

At the end of the season, Curry was the leading scorer in the country but was not among the stars showcased in the NCAA National Championship tournament. Davidson managed to secure a slot in the 2009 National Invitational Tournament – also known as the NIT – where they were the sixth seed. In the first round of the NIT on March 17, 2009, Curry made 9 of 19 field goals (47.4 percent) with 5 of 9 coming from the three-point distance to finish with 32 points. Despite turning the ball over 7 times, Davidson got the 70-63 win on the road at South Carolina.

Curry followed that performance with 26 points in the semifinals game at Saint Mary's on March 23, 2009, converting 11 of 27 from the field (40.7 percent) and 4 of 10 from three-point range along with 9 rebounds, 5 assists, and 2 steals. But

Davidson lost that game. Curry concluded his college career with his best numbers yet, sporting an average of 28.6 points per game. Curry also was named as NCAA All-American first-team player.

Stephen Curry chose to leave Davidson after his junior year. But it was not an easy decision for him to make. Some NBA players do not even hesitate to leave after one year in college. But McKillop said Curry was hesitant as he put a lot of effort into making his decision. Of course, the coach was the first to know the decision because he was one of the few people who had a lot of faith in Stephen. In his 104 total games at Davidson, Curry averaged 25.3 points, 4.5 rebounds, and 5.7 assists per game. His 2,635 total points and 414 total three-pointers are both Davidson records.

Leaving school was a smart move for him since he was already one of the best players in college basketball. He was all set to proceed to the NBA. In his college career, Curry had many highs and lows. He even went scoreless in a game, but this was due to the opposing coach assigning two defenders to him at all times. As a result, his teammates were often left with wide-open shots, and they still won that game.

In the end, Curry left Davidson as one of the best players, if not the very best, that the Wildcats had ever seen. He soon joined the NBA as a first round, seventh overall pick for the Golden State Warriors.

Chapter 4: NBA Career

"I've never been afraid of big moments. I get butterflies. I get nervous and anxious, but I think those are all good signs that I'm ready for the moment."

Stephen Curry

Curry made the right choice when he decided to claim eligibility for the 2009 NBA draft. He had reached the peak of college basketball and probably went down in history as Davidson's best basketball player ever. With numbers like his and experience from playing on the US U19 team, with whom Curry won a silver medal in 2007, he had boosted his chances of being selected as a top-10 draft pick.

He also managed to break some impressive records in his junior year of college, including the all-time scoring record for Davidson and the Southern Conference, school career records for free throws, three-pointers, 30-point games, 40-point games, and the single-season NCAA record for three-point field goals. Needless to say, Stephen Curry had a storied college career.

Stephen Curry came into the 2009 NBA draft standing about 6'3" and weighing 180 pounds. Though he was far from the incredibly scrawny kid that came into Davidson as a freshman, Stephen was still as skinny as he could get compared to the brawny and buff NBA players. From a physical standpoint, there was nothing about Curry that stood out. He was not all that tall. At 6'3", he had the right height for a point guard but was short for a shooting guard. He also was not very athletic and had a very average build.

As the NCAA's top scorer in his junior year in college, Stephen Curry was a lethal NBA player from the backcourt. Offensively, Stephen was the complete package as far as skills were concerned. Like his father, he attempted and made a lot of baskets from beyond the arc. His in-between game was not bad, either. Curry could get defenders off balance with his excellent ball-handling skills and could create shots from the perimeter in those situations.

First Year

The Golden State Warriors did not waste any time once Stephen Curry was drafted. They signed him to a four-year contract on July 8, 2009. The deal was estimated to be worth $13 million, which was slightly above the NBA rookie pay scale for that season. Golden State needed the help because they had one of their weakest rosters in recent years, and this proved to be an excellent opportunity for Curry to showcase his skills. As expected, Stephen came in as the starting point guard for the Warriors.

He arrived at the arena a little later than expected because of the heavy traffic. When he got there, NBA TV crewmen wanted to document his first game as an NBA player. Fans were also lining up to have autographs signed. At that level, Stephen was already receiving a lot of attention, though he was yet to play an NBA game. As a high pick in the first round of the draft, both the media and the fans expected a lot from him. Curry was then first in line as the Warriors were headed toward the court for their first entrance of the season. Curry did not disappoint, and he started his NBA campaign with high authority. He scored 14 points by converting 7 of 12 from the field, dished out 7 assists, and had 4 steals in his first appearance as a Warrior in a one-point loss, 108-107, to Houston on October 28, 2009.

After the game, Curry was vocal with his disappointment about the loss in his first-ever NBA game. He would also admit that he was very nervous yet, as always, he felt calm and natural on the hardwood floor. That was merely the first of 82 games on the calendar for Stephen Curry and the Golden State Warriors.

While he was starting, he was not getting a large bulk of the offensive opportunities, and there were a few games in which Curry scored in single digits. But, for the most part, he was scoring 10 to 19 points a game for the month of November before he got his first game with 20 or more points. He had played well enough as a rookie to become part of the 2009 All-Star event, participating in the three-point shootout held February 13, 2010, at American Airlines Center in Dallas, Texas. Curry also participated in the annual NBA Rookie Challenge, in which the NBA top rookies competed against second-year players in a special exhibition.

During the season, he became part of an elite group of players, including LeBron James and Dwyane Wade, with five or more 30-point, 5-assist games. Curry continued to develop as one of the league's best offensive threats, culminating in the regular-season finale on April 14, 2010, a 122-116 win on the road against the Portland Trail Blazers.

After Blake Griffin did not play in the 2009-10 NBA season due to injuries, Stephen Curry became a fan favorite for the Rookie of the Year (ROY) award. His only competitor was Tyreke Evans, mainly because of his ridiculous stats (Tyreke became one of only three other NBA players in history that averaged at least 20 points, 5 rebounds, and 5 assists). It was tough competing against such a stat line. Curry, on the other hand, finished the season with 17.5 points, 5.9 assists, 4.5

rebounds, and 2 steals per game.

That was enough to finish second in the ROY voting and to be a part of the All-Rookie First Team. He led all first-year players in assists, steals, and three-pointers made.

Curry's performance in his rookie season did not go unnoticed in NBA circles. Shortly after the end of the 2009-10 NBA regular season, he was selected for the U.S. national team. This came as a great comfort after he failed to qualify for the playoffs with the Warriors and did not win the Rookie of the Year award.

Though Stephen Curry's rookie season was better than expected, as he was arguably the second-best rookie of that season, there were a few setbacks that would have long-term effects on the rising star. After playing against the Lakers on March 15, Curry came to practice the following day. According to him, everything felt fine from the Laker game up until practice. However, when he woke up the next day, something was off.

Stephen woke up feeling some soreness in one of

his ankles. What was strange about it was that it was so sudden. He did not sprain it during the game against Los Angeles, or when he came to train the following day. Though it scared him at first, Stephen Curry tried to man up and went to the arena to play. He tried to get some shots off to try and get used to the soreness. However, Curry said that he could not even land on the ankle. That was after merely attempting two warm-up shots.

Curry had the team doctor check out his sore ankle. It appeared that the ankle was inflamed. Due to the injury, Stephen Curry had to sit out that game. It was a surprising setback for him, as he had planned on playing every game.

Though Curry came back healthy and without any serious ailments that season, the injured ankle would have bigger repercussions for his future. His NBA career almost went into limbo because of the long-term effects that lingered due to his ankle injuries.

Second Year

Curry picked up right where he left off during the Warriors' regular-season home opener on October 27, 2010, during a 132-128 win over the Houston Rockets. He made 9 of 16 field goals (56.3 percent), with 3 of 6 from three-point range, while recording a double-double with 25 points and 11 assists.

A little more than a week later, on November 8, 2010, Curry led the team with 34 points by making 12 of 21 from the field (57.1 percent) and all 8 free throws in a 109-102 win over the Toronto Raptors. This performance was quickly followed by 25 points, 8 assists, and 6 rebounds during a 122-117 win visiting the New York Knicks on November 10, 2010.

But the second-year player out of Davidson was still going to get his big games with the Golden State Warriors. On November 30, 2010, Curry led the team with 32 points, converting on 59.1 percent from the field to go along with 5 assists, 1 steal, and 1 block while Golden State lost at home to the San Antonio Spurs 118-98. In the first game of December 2010, the Warriors fell to the Oklahoma City Thunder by a score of 114-109 on December 5, 2010, despite Curry making 14 of 20 from the field (70 percent) while scoring 39 points.

Curry led the team in assists per game and started 74 games. The most he had in a single game was 13 assists, along with 23 points on 10 of 18 shooting (55.6 percent) from the field on February 13, 2011, during a 100-94 win over the Thunder. This was followed by 12 assists during Golden State's 103-93 loss at Atlanta on December 29, 2010.

Curry was also establishing himself as a great defensive player. During the Warriors' 120-90 loss on the road to the Chicago Bulls on November 11, 2010, Curry had a season-high 5 steals against Derrick Rose and others. There were four games in which Curry had 4 steals, including a 110-103 win on the road against the New Orleans Hornets on January 5, 2011, and again on January 21, 2011, during an 119-112 win over the Sacramento Kings. But Curry was still getting the job done on the other end of the court, as he made 12 of 21 from the field (57.1 percent) to score 34 points to go along with 12 rebounds.

Despite some good performances from the second-year point guard, the ankles began nagging him again. Curry suddenly sprained his right ankle yet again in a blowout loss to the San Antonio Spurs on December 8, 2010. It was apparent that Stephen had weak ankles because nobody had even touched him when he injured his ankle.

Stephen missed a bunch of games before coming back on Christmas Day. However, it seemed like the injuries had taken a toll on him, as he went 2 out of 15 from the field in that game. He did, however, have 11 assists in his return. Moreover, he did not suffer any more injuries to that ankle as the season went on.

Curry ended the season with an average of 18.6 points, 3.9 rebounds, 5.8 assists, 1.5 steals, and a 44.2 percent clip from three-point range.

Third Year and Injury

At the end of the 2010-11 season, Stephen Curry underwent surgery to repair torn ligaments in his right ankle, which had resulted from multiple sprains during his first two seasons in the NBA. Moreover, the purpose of the surgery was to strengthen the often-injured ankle.

Despite the extended rest period following the procedure to repair and strengthen the ailing right ankle, Stephen Curry found that nothing seemed to change. In a preseason game against the Sacramento Kings in the middle of December, Stephen was crossed over by rookie Jimmer Fredette. He was rushed to the locker room because he was in a lot of pain. It was a huge downer as he was just off a resting period after his ankle surgery.

But the very next day on December 26, 2011, Curry bounced back with 21 points, making 7 of 12 from the field and 6 of 7 free throws during a 99-91 win over the Chicago Bulls; he also had 10 assists to record a double-double.

Curry managed to appear in only 26 out of 66 games in the season due to his continued ankle problems. Curry sprained his ankle multiple times during the season and had to go through regular therapy. At that point, it looked as if Curry's career would go downhill because many other NBA stars failed to play at a stellar level after suffering chronic injuries.

Curry went in for a surgery hoping that he would be able to make a full recovery. Luckily for Stephen, there was no structural damage to his ankle. Cameras that went into his foot saw inflamed tissue and bone spurs that all came from the many times that Steph had sprained his ankle. What the doctor did was very simple. He removed all of those spurs from the foot. The original recovery time of six months, had the procedure been intrusive, was shortened to four months at most. Curry was ready for rehab in just three months after the surgery. Thanks to the doctor and his crew, the future face of basketball was saved.

After a disappointing 2011-12 NBA season and yet another failed attempt by the Warriors to qualify for the playoffs, Stephen Curry was back for the following season. The Golden State front office made some key moves during the offseason to change the team dynamic.

He also paired up with Klay Thompson in the backcourt, who had a promising rookie campaign, averaging 12.5 points, 2.4 rebounds, and 2.0 assists while playing about 24 minutes per game and converting on 44.3 percent from the field overall.

Curry looked as if he had real focus at the start of the 2012-2013 season, and there was great team chemistry under the guidance of Mark Jackson. That was immediately seen in Curry's game, even though he did not have the greatest of starts on October 31, 2012, in an 87-85 win at Phoenix.

He averaged more than 20 points per game in the first three months of the season and missed only five games due to ankle problems in January.

He exploded that February with averages of 25.4 points and 6.9 assists, starting on February 2, 2013, after missing a couple more games due to minor pains. In his first game back after a short break, Curry scored on 11 of 20 field goal attempts (55 percent), including 6 of 10 three-pointers, to finish with 29 points plus 8 assists, 2 rebounds, and 2 steals during an 113-93 win at home over the Phoenix Suns. Less than a week later, on February 8, 2013, the Warriors lost 99-93 on the road to the Memphis Grizzlies although Curry converted on 11 of 22 field goals and all 6 free throws to finish the game with 32 points, 8 assists, 5 rebounds, and 2 steals.

He had a monumental performance against the New York Knicks at Madison Square Garden in New York City, New York. He netted a career-high 54 points with 11 of 13 shooting from behind the three-point arc and 18 out of 28 overall from the field; he also had 7 assists, 6 rebounds, and 3 steals in the 109-105 loss on February 27, 2013.

Curry finished the 2012-2013 regular season averaging 22.9 points, 4 rebounds, 6.9 assists, and

1.6 steals while shooting with 45.3 percent accuracy from three-point land and 45.1 percent from the field overall. Curry won the Western Conference Player of the Month award for April, in which he averaged 25.4 points, 8.1 assists, 3.9 rebounds, and 2.1 steals with a field goal percentage of 46.5. He earned praise from Coach Mark Jackson for being half of the most intimidating backcourt shooting duo in NBA history, also known as the "Splash Brothers" (with Klay Thompson as the other half of the duo). This was the season when Curry became an All-Star quality guard and led the Warriors to their first playoff appearance in his era. They finished with a record of 47-35, which was good for second place in the Pacific Division behind the Los Angeles Clippers (56- 26). That gave them the sixth spot in the very competitive Western Conference playoffs.

Curry was selected as a starter for the 2014 NBA All-Star Game. It was his first appearance in his five-year career. Curry placed second behind Kevin Durant in fan voting for the Western Conference starters. It was a great accomplishment and a lot of buzz circulated a week before the game as everyone was talking about his sweet jump shot and three-point range. Even the President of the United States, Barack Obama, stated in an interview that Curry is the best shooter he has ever seen, including Chicago's South Side legends.

At the end of the first month of 2015, the 37-8 Warriors had a comfortable lead over their Western Conference rivals and had established themselves as the surprise team to beat in the West. Curry led the team in scoring in 19 of their total games and already had eight 30-plus scoring nights by January 2015.

He also led the Warriors in assists in all but five games up to that point. Stephen Curry had played in all of the Warriors' 45 regular-season games by January 31, 2015, and he was averaging 23.0 points, 8.1 assists, 4.7 rebounds, and 2.1 steals per game, all better than his career averages. He was also making three-pointers at a high 39.5 percent clip and was shooting a league-best 91.5% from the foul line heading into the midway point of the season.

As word of the Warriors' emergence spread, Stephen Curry's legend also started to grow. When the first set of fan votes for the 2015 NBA All-Star Games was announced, Curry topped the list for the Western Conference with 549,095 votes.

With the Golden State Warriors emerging as the league leader in the NBA team standings for the 2015 season, Stephen Curry's name began appearing in MVP discussions and deservedly so, because he was the motor that ran the best team in the league.

Curry became the Warriors' first MVP winner since Wilt Chamberlain in 1960, back when the Warriors were still playing for Philadelphia. He also became the second player in league history to win the MVP award and play for a team with 65 wins.

2015 NBA Finals

After opening the season with 20-to-1 odds to win the NBA title in the Las Vegas Superbook, the top-seeded Golden State Warriors started the 2015 postseason as the top title favorites, along with

LeBron James and his Cleveland Cavaliers.

The Western Conference finals series started on May 19, 2015. Curry took the lead for the team by making 13 of 22 field goals (6 of 11 from behind the three-point line) for a total of 34 points with 6 rebounds, 5 assists, and 2 steals in a close 110-106 win at home in the Oracle Arena. Curry made the final 9 points for Golden State, including the last two free throws in the final seconds to give the Warriors the 4-point lead with just four seconds left. In Game 2 on May 21, 2015, Curry sank 13 of 21 from the field, including 5 of 11 from behind the three-point line, for 33 points with 6 assists, 3 rebounds, and 1 steal in a 99- 98 win.

The third game of the series was not close at all. It was a 115-80 Golden State win on May 23, 2015, at the Toyota Center in Houston, Texas.

While Houston avoided the sweep in Game 4 with a 128-115 decision thanks to Harden's 45 points, the Warriors clinched the Western Conference title with a 104-90 win at home on May 27, 2015.

Winning the Western title set up a fascinating

NBA finals matchup between the young and offensive-powered Warriors against the Eastern Conference favorites, the Cleveland Cavaliers.

Curry had a good start in his NBA finals debut, sinking 10 of 20 from the field for 26 points, 8 assists, 4 rebounds, and 2 steals on June 4, 2015, during a 108-100 win at home.

But Cleveland evened the series by taking Game 2 on June 7, 2015, with a 95-93 win in Oakland. Golden State tied the series in Game 4 on June 11, 2015, when four players scored in double figures for the 103-82 win. Golden State returned home to Oakland and earned a 104-91 win on June 14, 2015. That win gave the Warriors the lead entering Game 6.

The Warriors made history by winning on June 16, 2015, by a score of 105-97 in Game 6 of the NBA finals. It was a great ending to a season after Golden State went 67-15 in the regular season – which was a franchise record –and won their first NBA championship since 1975.

For those who watched Curry struggle with

injuries in his first three seasons while Golden State missed the playoffs, it felt as if the organization's patience for their star athlete had paid off.

In a Sports Illustrated feature that ran after the NBA finals, Curry said winning the championship felt more special after the difficulties with his health and his ankles early in his career and being able to hold the championship trophy six years after starting his career in the NBA.

2015-16

Stephen Curry had already achieved so much. Stephen made his second NBA All-Star appearance. He was the most vital piece for the improvement of the Golden State Warriors. Stephen was one of the favorites for the Most Valuable Player award. The great shooter would eventually win the award by almost a landslide.

On his way to winning the award, Stephen Curry rearranged NBA history. He broke his record for most three-pointers made in a season. He converted a then-record of 286 made shots from beyond the arc. In addition to hitting the most three-pointers that season, Stephen Curry set the record for making 1,000 three-pointers in the shortest time.

Individual accolades are great, but what truly defined Stephen Curry's 2014-15 NBA season was the success the Golden State Warriors saw. The Warriors finished with a record of 67 wins against 15 losses. They had the best record in the NBA that season and were also the favorites for the NBA championship. As we know, Stephen and the Warriors went on to beat the Cleveland Cavaliers in six games to become the 2015 NBA champions.

But Stephen was not done carving his name into the record books of the NBA. Ever the hard worker, he went into the offseason with the same kind of work ethic and hunger that an NBA D-League player has when he's trying to make it on an NBA roster.

Only putting up jumpers from downtown a thousand times a day every night was no longer what Stephen Curry needed to improve his three-point shooting. As he normally did when he worked on his dribbling skills, Stephen needed to shock his body and his senses to force his body and his reflexes to adjust to new scenarios.

Instead of just shooting jump shots day and night in spot-up situations, Stephen Curry was made to shoot his long bombs from different positions and different distances from the floor. If Stephen Curry was not doing those shooting drills, he would shoot his usual set jump shots. Other than his jump shot, Curry further honed his already top-tier dribbling skills. With all those drills and workouts together with a Stephen Curry that had supreme confidence in his health coming into the 2015-16 NBA season, he was going to defend his MVP and his championship with more toys in his bag of tools and with more tricks up his sleeve.

A few hours after their championship banner was raised at Oakland's Oracle Arena, the Golden State

Warriors started a new season on October 27, 2015, with a 111-95 win over the New Orleans Pelicans. Curry made 14 of 26 from the field (53.8 percent), including 5 of 12 from three-point range (41.7 percent) to score 40 points in the first game of the NBA's 2015-16 season; he also collected 7 assists, 6 rebounds, and 2 steals. Curry and the rest of the Golden State Warriors were picking up right where they left off – winning games.

In fact, the Warriors won their first 24 games to start the regular season – a streak in which Curry averaged 32.5 points, 6.1 assists, 5.3 rebounds, and 2.1 steals. During that run, Curry's best individual game was easily on October 31, 2015, in a 134-120 win. It was ironic how Curry continued to be a nightmare for the New Orleans Pelicans on Halloween night. After shooting 63 percent from the field (17 of 27) featuring 57.1 percent from three-point range (8 of 14) and a perfect 11 for 11 from the foul line, Curry finished the game with 53 points, 9 assists, 4 rebounds, and 4 steals.

Curry had his first double-double of the NBA

season on November 6, 2015, during a 119-104 win at home against the Denver Nuggets in which he led the team, again, with 34 points and 10 assists; he also added 7 rebounds, 3 steals, and 1 block in the game. Curry was also close to hitting the 50-point mark on November 12, 2015, during a 129-116 win on the road against the Minnesota Timberwolves – he made 15 of 25 from the field (60 percent) and 61.5 percent from long distance to have 46 points, 5 rebounds, 4 assists, and 2 steals.

As the Warriors continued to go through November without losing a game, the competition got a lot harder, and there seemed to be pressure about when the streak was going to end. On November 30, 2015, the Warriors played the Utah Jazz in a very close road contest where Curry broke a 101-101 tie with a 26-foot field goal for 3 points in the final minute and sank two more free throws for security in the final seconds to give Golden State the 106-103 win. Curry led the team with 26 points, making 45 percent from the field while collecting 6 rebounds, 5 assists, and 2 steals.

They had the longest winning streak to begin a season in league history and the third longest overall. But, as with all good things, an end was inevitable. However, the team that defeated them might have been a surprise, as the Warriors lost on the road to the Milwaukee Bucks on December 12, 2015. The win elevated the Bucks to 10-15 at the time. While Curry made 45.5 percent from the field for 28 points, he was not effective from long range as he made just 2 out of 9 (22.2 percent) three-point attempts while collecting 7 rebounds and 5 assists.

A few days later, on December 18, 2015, Golden State exacted some revenge against the Milwaukee Bucks with a 121-112 win at their home court at the Oracle Arena. Curry nearly had a triple-double with 26 points, 10 rebounds, and 9 assists while making 50 percent of his field goals and 10 of 11 from the foul line. A little more than a week later, Curry got another triple-double on December 28, 2015, with 23 points, 14 rebounds, and 10 assists, hitting 43.8 percent of his field goal attempts (6 of

13 from three-point range) to help the Warriors get the 122-103 win at home over the Sacramento Kings.

The Warriors suffered their second loss of the season on December 30, 2015, a 114-91 defeat on the road by the Dallas Mavericks in a game where Curry did not play because of an injury to his left shin that he suffered during the win over the Sacramento Kings.

Curry tried his best to fight against his injury and play but was only able to play for a few minutes in the next 5 games. Curry continued to fight through the pain during the team's 109-88 win over the Los Angeles Lakers, in which he made 6 of 13 field goals (4 of 8 from three-point land) for 17 points with 6 assists and 3 steals.

Curry had some struggles during the next four weeks, as in the team's 128-108 win over the Portland Trail Blazers on January 8, 2016. In that game, he made just 8 of 18 from the field (44.4 percent) and only 4 of 11 from the three-point distance (36.4 percent) to score 26 points with 9 assists, 3 rebounds, and 1 steal.

On January 9, 2016, during a 128-116 win over the Sacramento Kings, Curry led the Warriors with 38 points, 11 assists, 6 rebounds, 1 steal, and 1 block while making 57.1 percent from the field (12 of 21) and an equal percentage from three-point range (8 of 14). Curry followed that up with 31 points and 6 assists during the Warriors' 111-103 win over the Miami Heat. Curry had another great game with 38 points, 9 assists, 5 rebounds, 3 steals, and 1 block while making 13 of 25 field goals (52 percent), but just 5 of 12 from three-point range (41.7 percent) in a 112-110 loss to the Denver Nuggets on January 13, 2016. It was only the third loss Golden State had suffered all season. The Warriors bounced back rather quickly with a 116-98 win at home over the Los Angeles Lakers on January 14, 2016. Curry made 9 of 18 from the field, with most of his shots taken from the three-point distance (8 of 16). He finished the game with 26 points, 6 rebounds, 3 assists, and another steal.

Golden State went on another winning streak to conclude the first half of the NBA season before the 2016 NBA All-Star Game. It started on January 18, 2016, when the Warriors earned a blowout win on the road over the Cleveland Cavaliers, 132-98. Curry made 12 of 18 from the field (66.7 percent) and 7 of 12 from three-point range (58.3 percent) while making all 4 of his free throws for 35 total points to go along with 5 rebounds, 4 assists, and 3 steals. Curry then had a double-double with 25 points and 11 assists while collecting 7 rebounds, 2 steals, and 1 block as Golden State defeated the Chicago Bulls on the road on January 20, 2016. Curry made 8 of 18 from the field (44.4 percent) and a perfect 6 of 6 on the foul line. Two nights later, on January 22, 2016, Curry recorded his second triple-double of the season. He made 8 of 15 from behind the three-point arc (53.3 percent) to give him 39 points with 12 assists and 10 rebounds in the team's 40th win of the season over the Indiana Pacers, 122-110.

The streak continued January 25, 2016, against the team with the second-best record in the

Western Conference, the San Antonio Spurs. The Warriors' defense held the Spurs to just 41.9 percent from the field, with the team led by Kawhi Leonard's 16 points while the others struggled. On the other side, Curry made 12 of 20 from the field (60 percent), including 6 of 9 from behind the three-point arc (66.7 percent), and converted 7 of 7 from the foul line to score 37 points; he also had 5 steals.

Curry was not responsible for all of the game-winning shots. On January 30, 2016, during a road game against the Philadelphia 76ers – who were just 7-40 going into the contest – the game was tied at 105-105 before Draymond Green passed to the open Harrison Barnes for a 23-foot basket with one second left that gave Golden State a 108-105 win. Curry still had an efficient game, making 9 of 19 from the field (47.4 percent) for 23 points, 6 assists, 5 rebounds, 2 blocks, and 1 steal in a little more than 34 minutes. Curry had one of his worst shooting performances with just 29.4 percent from the field for only 13 points during a 116-95 win on the road against the New York Knicks on January

31, 2016. But Thompson led the Warriors with 34 points while Green had a triple-double with 20 points, 10 rebounds, and 10 assists – the first of many for Green.

Then again, Curry is a reigning NBA MVP for a reason, and he showed why on February 3, 2016, during another road win against the Washington Wizards, 134-121. He made 19 of 28 from the field (67.9 percent) and was most effective from behind the three-point arc by sinking 11 of 15 (73.3 percent) for a total of 51 points. He also had 7 rebounds, 3 steals, and 2 assists, while Green had another triple-double with 12 points, 12 assists, and 10 rebounds. Curry followed that up with a double-double of his own with 26 points and 10 assists to go along with 6 rebounds and 3 steals in a 116-108 win over Oklahoma City Thunder on February 6, 2016. Curry could have had more points, but made only 10 of 26 from the field (38.5 percent) and only 1 of 9 from three-point range.

In the final games before the All-Star break, Curry continued to prove that he was one of the league's best players by making 7 of 16 from three-point distance and 12 of 24 overall for 35 points, 9 assists, 5 rebounds, and 1 steal. This was during Golden State's 123-110 win at home over the Houston Rockets on February 9, 2016. One night later, on the road against the Phoenix Suns on February 10, 2016, Curry played only 30 minutes. He made 9 of 17 from the field (52.9 percent) and half of his attempts from three-point distance for 26 points while collecting 9 rebounds and 9 assists to help the Warriors get the win.

The win over the Phoenix Suns elevated the Golden State Warriors to a record of 48-4 to lead the entire NBA with the best record. It also put them ahead of schedule in their efforts to surpass the 72 wins that the 1995-96 Chicago Bulls amassed to set the record for victories in a single season.

Curry had missed only two games at this point in the season and had averaged 29.8 points, 6.6 rebounds, 5.3 rebounds, and 2.1 steals in what turned out to be another MVP season. He had also converted 50.8 percent of his field goal attempts (45.4 percent from three-point range), and he was on pace to have the best season of his career –his highest scoring average came in the 2013-14 season when he scored 24 points per game. In his MVP season, Curry averaged a little under that, with 23.8 points per game.

Chapter 5: Personal Life

"Everything happens for a reason, and everything has a story, and if you take time to realize what your dream is and what you really want in life... whether it's sports, whether it's in other fields, you have to realize that there's always work to do."

Stephen Curry

It is a well-known fact that Stephen is one of three children of former NBA sharpshooter, Dell Curry. Not everybody knows that his mother Sonya played volleyball at Virginia Tech, and was considered the team's star at the time.

His siblings are involved with sports as well. His brother Seth was part of Duke University's basketball squad for three seasons and his sister Sydel Curry plays volleyball at Elon University. The Curry family developed tight bonds over the years, and the fact that Dell Curry resigned as an assistant coach of the Charlotte Bobcats before the start of the 2007 NBA season so that he could watch his son's college games is proof of that commitment. Dell has also praised his son, saying that he is very proud to have watched Stephen grow up and play the game that he played and that his son is even better than he was.

Stephen's younger brother, Seth, accomplished one feat that Stephen did not manage to do. He played for the Duke Blue Devils, regarded as having one of the best college basketball programs in the country. Seth was part of Duke's program while in college for three full seasons after he transferred from a small program at Liberty University. Even though he averaged 17.5 points on 46.5% shooting, Seth went undrafted in 2013 and has played here and there on different NBA teams since then, most recently playing 44 games for the Sacramento Kings in the 2015-2016 NBA season and currently with the Dallas Mavericks. An injury suffered during his last season at Duke hurt Seth's draft stock. He played a preseason game for the Golden State Warriors, and he spent

30 seconds on the floor together with his brother. After that, Seth was a D-League standout, averaging 23.8 points per game, and was a member of the 2014-2015 D-League All-Star teams, biding his time until an NBA franchise took notice of him. Seth had a short stint with the Orlando Magic in the 2014 2015 preseason, before continuing to play in the D-League for the Erie BayHawks. In the 2015-2016 seasons, Seth got his first big break on July 22 when he signed a two-year, $2 million guaranteed deal with the Kings.

Stephen's mother taught him the importance of finishing his education while he was young. During the NBA lockout in 2011, while his colleagues were busy touring, or finding overseas jobs or fancy internships, Stephen went back to college at Davidson. He enrolled in courses with the objective of finishing his sociology degree. He reunited with Coach McKillop and practiced with the basketball team whenever he could, offering them input from a unique perspective. He even worked on a senior research project about NBA players' tattoos and how it relates to their public image, tabbing former teammates Monta Ellis and Anthony Morrow as his primary sources.

Background of Parents

Stephen Curry is the son of Dell Curry and Sonya Adams. Dell Curry is a former NBA shooting guard who was well-known for his great shooting eye. It all started while he was growing up in Harrisonburg, Virginia, and his coach at Fort Defiance High School helped him by providing quite a unique practice area – a barn. It was either that or shooting hoops by using a goal that was attached to a tree in his family's yard. He spent a few hours every day practicing in the barn and even set a goal of making as many as 500 shots in one practice. It paid off, as he finished his high school career as the highest-scoring player in Fort Defiance history and was one of the stars showcased in the 1982 McDonald's High School All-American game.

Additionally, Dell was offered a chance to play

professional baseball, a sport he also enjoyed in high school. However, he passed on the opportunity after he was selected by the Texas Rangers in the 1982 major league baseball draft. Dell chose to go to Virginia Tech University, where he continued to play baseball in the spring. But the winter months were for basketball, and that seemed to be his true calling, even after the Baltimore Orioles drafted him in the 1985 MLB Draft. While he was okay in baseball, with a 3.81 ERA as a pitcher during his collegiate career, he was much better suited for the game of basketball at 6- foot-4 and about 190 pounds.

Right off the bat, Dell made an impact on a Hokies team that appeared in the National Invitational Tournament in 1983 and 1984, when that event was considered second only to the NCAA National Championship tournament. In his freshman season, Dell averaged 14.5 points, 3.3 assists, 3 rebounds, and almost 2 steals per game and the Virginia Tech Hokies finished with a 23- 11 record.

Dell had a good season as a junior with averages of

18.2 points, 5.8 rebounds, 3.1 assists, and 2.4 steals. But it was in his senior season that Dell made a national impact on a team that finished 22-9 and won another berth in the 1986 NCAA tournament – averaging collegiate career highs of 24.1 points, 6.8 rebounds, 3.8 assists, and 2.6 steals.

Overall, Dell finished second on the all-time list at Virginia Tech with 2,389 points and claimed the school record for steals with 295. It was a career that earned him the opportunity to play in the National Basketball Association after he was selected 15th overall in the league's 1986 draft by the Utah Jazz.

His rookie year in Utah did not give him more than about 9½ minutes in each of his 67 appearances, and he averaged about 4.9 points in that span. The Jazz decided to trade Dell to the Cleveland Cavaliers, where his average minutes increased to about 19 per game. That led to his averaging about 10 points per game for a team that barely made the NBA Playoffs with a record of 42-

40; the Cavaliers fell quickly in the first round of the Eastern Conference Playoffs to the Chicago Bulls.

Dell then became eligible for the NBA's expansion draft to start the 1988-89 season and was picked by the Charlotte Hornets. During his first four seasons with the Hornets, Dell had some of the best numbers of his career, including averages of 16 points and about 1.5 steals in the 1989-90 season. The best year of his NBA career was the 1993-94 season when he averaged 16.3 points, 3.2 rebounds, 2.7 assists, and 1.2 steals.

Dell played for Charlotte for 10 seasons before spending a season with the Milwaukee Bucks and three with the Toronto Raptors, with his averages steadily declining before he retired in 2002. After a total of 16 seasons, Dell finished with 12,670 points, 2,617 rebounds, and 1,909 assists.

Stephen's mother was a prolific volleyball player who grew up in Radford, Virginia, and made a name for herself as a basketball and volleyball star, helping Radford High School win state championships in both sports. This led to her earning a scholarship to play volleyball for Virginia Tech in 1984.

She found her success on the volleyball court, earning a spot on the All- Metropolitan League team and leading the nation in volleyball aces. During that time, she met Dell on the campus of Virginia Tech, and the couple got married in 1988.

Faith and Spirituality

Stephen Curry grew up with devout Christian parents in a household where a morning family devotional time was a must. Curry stated in an interview that he gave himself to Christ in the fourth grade at the Central Church of God in Charlotte. His parents continued to support his faith and made sure that he fully understood his commitment. He is now one of the best young players in the NBA and a leader of a playoff squad, but he is a devoted husband and father as well.

Now he has transferred his work ethic, attitude

toward the game, and personal values into his NBA career. He stated in an interview that he felt that God wanted to use him in the league to show that not all successful athletes live the celebrity lifestyle that comes with all the money and fame.

An interesting fact about Curry is that he always writes biblical verses on his shoes. Some of his favorites include Philippians 4:13 and Romans 8:28 (which is also his mother's favorite).

"It represents a Bible verse I wear on my shoe. Philippians 4:13. It says 'I can do all things through Christ who strengthens me.' It's also my mantra, how I get up for games and why I play the way I do." - Stephen Curry

Marriage

On July 30, 2011, Stephen married his high school sweetheart, Ayesha Alexander, whom he had met in a church youth group when he was 15. After finishing high school, Ayesha decided to pursue her acting career in Los Angeles where she had roles in the "Whittaker Bay" and "Hannah Montana" television series.

Stephen went to a basketball camp on the West Coast and contacted her through Facebook for the first time after high school, and the rest is history. The couple has two daughters: Riley, born in 2011, and Ryan, born in 2015. On the day of their wedding, the couple asked that all guests donate funds to the Thanks USA organization instead of bringing wedding gifts. The organization supports the families of the United States military personnel.

He is a very dedicated and loving husband to his wife Ayesha and father to their daughters Riley and Ryan.

Golf

An interesting fact about Stephen is that he also loves to play golf. Stephen considers it to be his second sport. At one point, there was even a news article that explored why he did not want to play in Minnesota, and one of the main reasons was the bad golf weather out there. He later laughed that off as an inaccurate statement and said that he can always find the time and place for a good game of golf.

Chapter 6: Legacy and Future

"On the court, I'm not afraid of anything. I try to have confidence and have a belief in myself."

Stephen Curry

Stephen Curry transformed Davidson College. Curry's three seasons at Davidson will be remembered for many generations to come. He is one of only six players in Davidson history who made it to the NBA and the first after Brandon Williams, who played for the Warriors in the 1997-98 NBA season.

His basketball exploits are not the only reason that Curry is still beloved at Davidson. Many teammates, schoolmates, and team staff members gush about his positive attitude and friendliness toward everyone. They all claim that his fame has not changed who he is as a person, that he is still very humble and approachable, just as he was in college.

Even though he had NBA genes, Stephen Curry did not enter college basketball as a top prospect. He developed into a scoring machine at Davidson and, as much as he received from the school, he also gave back a lot. After being rejected by a couple of NCAA Division teams, Curry decided to enroll at Davidson.

Curry has also proven that he is more than just a deadly shooter and scorer. In the eyes of many coaches and fellow players, he is one of the most complete point guards in the league.

When he won the 2015 MVP while breaking his three-point record on the way, many people began claiming that Stephen has already become the greatest shooter in NBA history at this early point in his career. But, Curry just about silenced all of his doubters when he was shocking millions of spectators with the distance he had been shooting his three-pointers and the way he had been putting up his outside shots in the 2015-16 season. Because Stephen Curry is the only player in NBA history to have made at least 400 three-pointers in a single season, you can no longer argue with the fact that he is already the greatest shooter in basketball history.

Stephen Curry's volume of three-point shots made is not the only thing that solidifies him as the NBA's greatest shooter. It is the quality of the shots he has been making that puts him at a level above the other shooters the league has seen. However, the biggest way in which Stephen Curry changed the game of basketball was through his shooting. In today's NBA game, teams have been utilizing the three-point shot more than ever. It has become the ultimate weapon for any team today.

As of this moment, we may already have an idea of where Stephen Curry's career is going, barring injuries. He is going to be known as the best shooter in NBA history without a doubt. He has a chance of cementing his place as the best player in Golden State franchise history. He has a chance of winning more titles and more MVPs, especially with how awesome he has been playing and with how great the Golden State Warriors have been playing as a team. However, Curry's on-court achievements and championships will not be the only factors to define his legacy as a player.

What will define Stephen Curry's legacy is how he has changed and will change the game of basketball.

Conclusion

Thank you for choosing this book and I hope that it was an interesting read for you.

The story of Stephen Curry is an inspiring one and it goes on to prove that even if the odds are stacked against you, you can still win. He struggled against many biases in the basketball world with regards to his build and height but now he's known as the most dangerous shooter of all time.

Curry is still playing for the Golden State Warriors and taking them with him on the path to glory. He's broken numerous records throughout his career and will definitely be remembered as a great legend of basketball.

88743980R00055

Made in the USA
Columbia, SC
03 February 2018